Tricks & Stunts to fool your friends

by Sheila Anne Barry
illustrated by Doug Anderson

 Sterling Publishing Co. Inc. New York

Thank you—Lincoln Boehm (for the idea), Charles Nurnberg (for your wisdom and help), Esther Nelson, my dear friend (for sharing your excellent material), David Boehm, my editor (for his great good sense), and Burton Hobson for making everything possible.

Library of Congress Cataloging in Publication Data

Barry, Sheila Anne.
  Tricks & stunts to fool your friends.

  Includes index.
  Summary: Chapter titles include: "It Can't Be Done,"
"Ghoulish and Foolish," "Sneaky Numbers," "Mind-Reading
Tricks," and "Card Tricks."
  1. Tricks—Juvenile literature. [1. Tricks]
I. Anderson, Doug, 1919–   ill. II. Title.
III. Title: Tricks and stunts to fool your friends.
GV1548.B37   1984   793.8   84-87
ISBN 0-8069-4694-6
ISBN 0-8069-7856-2 (pbk.)
ISBN 0-8069-4695-4 (lib. bdg.)

Some of the material in this book appeared in *Super-Colossal Book of Puzzles, Tricks & Games* by Sheila Anne Barry, copyright © 1978 by Sterling Publishing Co., Inc. That material was adapted in part from the following books, all of them © Sterling Publishing Co., Inc., unless otherwise indicated: Rudolf Dittrich, *Tricks & Games for Children* © 1964; Lillian and Godfrey Frankel, *101 Best Games for Girls* © 1952; Walter B. Gibson, *Junior Magic* © 1963 Doubleday, 1977 Walter B. Gibson; Muriel Mandell, *Games to Learn By* © 1958, 1972; Peggy and Robert Masters, *101 Best Stunts and Novelty Games* © 1954; Norvin Pallas, *Calculator Puzzles, Tricks & Games* © 1976; Ib Permin, *Hokus Pokus* © 1969; Walter Sperling, *How to Make Things Out of Paper* © 1961.

Third Printing, 1985

Copyright © 1984 by Sterling Publishing Co., Inc.
Two Park Avenue, New York, N.Y. 10016
Distributed in Australia by Capricorn Book Co. Pty. Ltd.
Unit 5C1 Lincoln St., Lane Cove, N.S.W. 2066
Distributed in the United Kingdom by Blandford Press
Link House, West Street, Poole, Dorset BH15 1LL, England
Distributed in Canada by Oak Tree Press Ltd.
% Canadian Manda Group, P.O. Box 920, Station U
Toronto, Ontario, Canada M8Z 5P9
Manufactured in the United States of America

Contents

Introduction

What do the tricks and stunts in this book have in common?

Probably the most important thing is the unique ability to amaze and delight the people you show them to. (Some of them will continue amazing and delighting you, too, no matter how many times you perform them.)

None of them calls for elaborate preparations or equipment (which takes the joy out of doing any trick) or for sleight-of-hand (which takes so much practice). You can perform most of these tricks for friends or family at a moment's notice.

They don't depend on puns and word play. None of these are phony tricks that leave you disappointed.

The card tricks don't call for fake decks or marking the cards. Most of the card tricks in this collection work by themselves—as if by magic.

In fact, some of the tricks here seem so mysterious that you could use them in a magic act, if you wanted to. But they cover a much wider range than that. Some are "betchas." Some are based on biological or physical oddities. Some are famous classics and others are practically unknown. But they are all superb tricks—the very best foolers we've ever found.

They come from a large number of sources: from long forgotten, long out-of-print collections, from the files of magicians, even from science texts! Others come from someone's grand-aunt or dad, from a dancing teacher, an engineer, an actor. That's one of the great bonuses of performing these super-foolers: sometime you'll be doing a trick for a couple of friends and suddenly their eyes will light up, and they'll tell you about a trick they learned years ago that stuck in their memories—and go on to show it to you, too! That's the best kind!

Many of the tricks and stunts in this book have been collected in just that way. They're all intriguing and easy to do. They're all surprising in some way, and there's a kind of wonder about them, even when you understand how or why they work. Have fun with them—and pass them along!

1. It Can't Be Done!

All the tricks in this chapter deal with simple, everyday actions you and your friends have done hundreds of times. But there's a catch: For some reason, you won't be able to do them. That reason may have to do with the odd way the human body works—or it may have to do with trickery of the lowest kind! Some of the stunts are amazing. Some will drive your friends wild. But they're the most intriguing tricks we've ever found that
NO ONE CAN DO.

You Can't Lift Your Foot

In the room you're in right now there's a spot in which you won't be able to lift your foot. No one will hold you down—or touch your foot or any other part of you. You won't be glued down—but you still won't be able to lift your foot off the ground. Want to bet?

Stand with your head, shoulder, side and heel tight against the wall. Then try to lift your outside leg without moving any part of your body away from the wall.

It can't be done—no matter how strong you are. Moving that foot throws you off balance and your body automatically moves away from the wall to keep you from falling down.

You Can't Pick Up a Coin

There's a coin on the floor of the room you're in, but you can't pick it up. No one will stop you. No one will pick it up first. It's not bolted or glued to the floor. But you still won't be able to pick it up. Try it.

Stand with your back to the wall, touching it with your head and your heels. Have someone put a coin on the floor in front of you. Now try to get the coin without moving your heels.

It can't be done: Your position at the wall makes it impossible for you to bend over and get the coin without losing your balance and falling over.

You Can't Jump

There's a spot in the room where you won't be able to jump. You'll be standing. No one will hold you back in any way or put anything on your head. But you won't be able to get off the ground. Why?

Stand with your back to the wall, touching it with head, hips and heels. You can't jump up without moving away from the wall—for the same reason as before.

You Can't Write "TENNESSEE"

You'll have a pencil and paper. You can sit at a table to write. No one and nothing will touch your hands. But you still won't be able to write a simple word like "TENNESSEE." How come?

Before you start, practice a little foot movement—a simple circling of one foot under the table. Move your foot clockwise in a circle about as big as a plate. (When you try this on your friends, sit down and demonstrate the motion for them.)

As soon as you get used to that motion, take up the pencil and try to write "TENNESSEE." Don't stop the movement for a second while you're writing. No matter how hard you try, you won't be able to write anything but strange-looking hieroglyphics.

The secret is that it's difficult to keep two very different motions going at the same time. Your hand wants to make the same movements that your foot is making. But look out: With practice you'll be able to master this one—and so will your victims!

You Can't Open Your Fingers

Once you put your fingertips together—in a certain position—you won't be able to move them apart. Hard to believe?

Bend your fingers and put your hands together so that your fingers meet, as in Illustration 1.

Illus. 1

Move out your third fingers (the tall ones) on each hand, so that they point up and lean against each other. Get the rest of your fingers tightly joined again, as in the illustration below.

Illus. 2

Now try to separate your third fingers—without separating any of the others.

Can't be done!

Money Won't Slip
Through Your Fingers

You'll hold a coin with your fingers, and you won't be able to let go of it. No, it won't be glued to your hand or tied on. No one will touch it—or you. But you won't be able to drop the coin. Do you believe it?

Put your hands together so that your fingertips meet, except for the third fingers (the tall ones) of each hand, which are clasped. Ask someone to slip a coin between your fourth fingertips (the ring finger), as in the illustration.

Now try to open your fingers enough to drop the coin, without changing the positions of your other fingers.

You can't do it—unless you separate your other fingertips.

EXTRA: You can do this trick by clasping your pinkies instead of your third fingers. In either case, you won't be able to "open" your fourth fingertips enough to drop the coin.

The reason this trick works either way is that the fourth finger is the weakest one. It doesn't have muscles as strong as the others, and it depends on the fingers alongside for its strength. If they can't come to its aid, it is helpless.

And Won't Brush Off Your Hand

Put a small coin right in the center of your palm. Now try to brush it off with your hair brush (or a clothes brush). You won't be able to do it—at least, not if you use regular brushing motions.

Why? That hollow in your palm is deeper than you think, and the usual brush strokes will never sweep the coin away.

You Can't Fold a Paper in Half 10 Times

No matter what size the sheet of paper is—even if it's a double sheet of the largest newspaper in town—you won't be able to fold it in half 10 times.

There's no catch: You'll see why if you think about what happens as you fold the paper. The first time you fold you'll get 2 sheets; the second time, 4 sheets; the third, 8 sheets; the fourth, 16 sheets; the fifth, 32 sheets; the sixth, 64 sheets, the seventh, 128 sheets (the number of sheets in this book)!

If you could manage to fold it the eighth and ninth times, you'd be folding 512 sheets at the same time! Want to try for 10?

You Will Never Be Left with the Last Straw

You can play this game with drinking straws, or toothpicks or sticks. If you play it with straws, use four of them, each cut into four parts, so that you have sixteen pieces. Place the straws in one straight line on the table. Now challenge a friend to play against you.

The rules are simple: The two of you take turns removing 1, 2 or 3 straws at a time from the line. The one who gets the last straw loses. You will *never* be left with the last straw if you go first—and probably, you'll be able to win even if you don't go first. Here's the secret:

Take 3 straws, leaving 13.
At your next turn, leave 9 straws.
At your next turn, leave 4 straws.
At your next turn, leave 1 straw.

Those are the numbers to remember: 13, 9, 4 and 1.

If you have to let your opponent start, still try to get to these combinations. You may still win, if your opponent hasn't figured out the secret.

No One Is Strong Enough to Lift You Up

The lifting up is done by the elbows, by a person who stands facing you. But even though the person may weigh a hundred pounds more than you do—and be a weightlifter—he or she won't be able to pick you up. You can bet on it.

If you keep your elbows by your sides, lined up with your body, it will be easy to lift you up. But if you angle them forward (as in the illustration), so that your arms and elbows are no longer in line with your center of gravity (and keep them loose and relaxed), it will be very tough for anyone to get you off the ground.

No One Can Beat You at the Toothpick Game

This game is similar to the last one: the loser is the one with the last toothpick, straw or stick, and only two can play. Start by placing 12 toothpicks on the table in 3 rows:

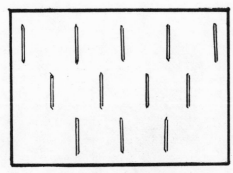

The starting set up: 12 toothpicks in 3 rows

top row: 5 toothpicks
middle row: 4 toothpicks
bottom row: 3 toothpicks

Each player is allowed to take as many toothpicks as he or she wants from any *one* row at a time. You will always win.

HOW IT IS DONE: When your opponent goes first, it doesn't matter much what he or she does. Try to leave any of these combinations after your turn:

1. 2 rows of equal numbers
2. rows of 1, 2, and 3 toothpicks
3. rows of 5, 4 and 1 toothpicks
4. rows of 1, 1 and 1.

16

If your opponent takes two toothpicks on the first turn from the bottom row, leaving you with rows of 5, 4, and 1, he or she can win, but most players don't know that.

If you have to go first, you're sure to win if you take 2 from the bottom row. But if you don't want to give away the secret by making that move, take 1 from the bottom row—or 2 from the middle row—or 3 from the top row. These are the most confusing moves and will probably allow you to get back to a winning combination on your next turn.

Why are those four combinations winners? If you leave 2 equal rows (of 3 each, let's say) and your opponent takes 1, you take 1 from the other row, leaving 2 equal rows again. Now, if your opponent takes 2, you take 1, leaving the last toothpick. If your opponent takes 1, you take 2, leaving the last toothpick again.

Suppose you leave 1, 2 and 3 toothpicks. If your opponent takes 3, you take 2, leaving the last. If your opponent takes 2, you take 3, leaving the last. If your opponent takes the row of 1, you take 1 from the row of 3, leaving 2 equal rows of 2, and you win—as described in the last paragraph.

If you leave 5, 4 and 1, you can always convert the next step into 2 equal rows of 1, 1 and 1—or 1, 2 and 3—and win.

You Can't Hold Up a Glass of Water

This trick is supposed to have originated in a seaport where sailors and dock hands were showing off how strong they were. One boasted that he could rip a thick telephone book in half, while another bragged about his ability to bend iron bars. A third claimed that he could keep an automobile from moving by holding it back with his hands.

A bystander suggested that he knew of a feat of strength that no one could do. All of the strong men were eager to show their strength, but they were surprised when the bystander brought them a glass full of water.

"Hold this glass on the palm of your hand for seven minutes," he said, "and keep your arm stretched out straight all the time."

The first man shook so much that the glass fell to the ground and broke before the seven minutes were up. The second got a cramp in his arm, and the third gave up in disgust.

Supposedly, no one has ever held the glass for seven minutes. A few people claim to have done it—but they haven't offered any proof. Try it yourself!

You Can't Stand Up

You're sitting in a perfectly ordinary straight-backed chair in a perfectly ordinary position. But you can't get up.

No one is holding you down. You're not tied up. You're not hypnotized. How did you get stuck?

Here's the catch: When you sit in the chair, keep your feet together, flat on the floor in front of you. Keep your back straight, touching the back of the chair. Your hands should be in your lap. Your problem is to stand without moving your feet or moving your back away from the chair. You'll never do it.

Why? In order to stand up, you have to get your weight and your feet in line with each other. That means that in order to get up from your chair, you either have to:

1. Move your body forward over your feet (and you can't do that because you have to keep your back against the chair) or
2. Move your feet backwards under the chair in line with your body (and you can't do that because you have to keep your feet flat on the ground).

Your friends won't believe this trick until they try it, because most of us make those balancing moves automatically, without thinking about them at all.

The Unburstable Balloon

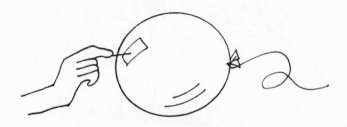

Your friends probably think it's easy to burst a balloon, especially with a pin. But you have a balloon that won't break—even though you jab it, again and again, with a pin.

Before you do this trick, place a small piece of transparent cellophane tape on the balloon. When you stick the balloon with the pin, jab it into the tape, which is made of stronger stuff than the balloon. Air will leak out, but the balloon won't pop!

Not So Macho

Your tallest, beefiest, most macho male friend won't be able to lift up a chair that the daintiest, tiniest female can lift with no problem. Impossible? Try this:

Have your dainty female friend—Suzi—face the wall and take four steps backwards, each step about the length of her shoe. Put a chair in front of her, but not touching the wall. Now ask her to lean over the chair, place her forehead against the wall, and lift the chair. She'll do it, with no difficulty.

Now ask your macho friend—Rex—to do the same thing. To his horror, he won't be able to budge it!

The secret? Those steps backwards that Suzi and Rex took put them in different places. Suzi's feet are smaller in relation to her height than Rex's are. Besides that, she's probably wearing sleeker, less bulky shoes. As a result, she's closer to the chair than Rex, and in a good position to pick it up.

Rex, however, is far enough away from the chair to be slightly off balance when he leans over it. And, in that position, he can't do the task.

Note: Pushing the chair against the wall is not allowed.

2. Ghoulish and Foolish

Every trick in this chapter has something odd about it. It may be something strange and scary—or just something peculiar—or simply something that's mystifying. But they're all fun. Ghouls especially will like them.

You Have a Rubber Thumb

Hold one thumb straight up and grasp it tightly with your other hand (see Illustration 1).

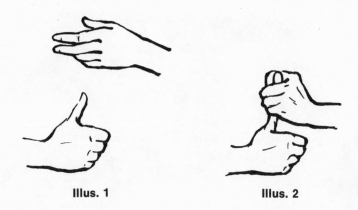

Illus. 1   **Illus. 2**

Illustration 2 shows how this trick looks from the front. The thumb of the top hand is shoved under the index finger of that hand. When the end peeks out, it looks as if it's the end of the thumb on your *lower* hand.

First get into the position in Illustration 1. Then bring your hands together and start "pulling" on the lower thumb, making faces as if you're in great pain. Actually, you're not pulling at all. All you're doing is moving your upper hand slowly up the thumb which is being "stretched."

Wiggle your lower hand back and forth with great effort, and slowly slip the end of your upper thumb under your index finger so that it peeks out at the top.

"Stretch" your thumb as far as you can without giving yourself away. As soon as the end of your lower thumb starts to appear, slide your upper hand all the way back down to the lower hand with a sudden jerk—as if the stretched thumb were snapping back into place. Then open your hand quickly and begin massaging the "rubber" thumb as though you can still feel the pain.

Practice the trick in front of a mirror until you get the impression yourself that your thumb is being stretched.

Younger spectators will be especially pleased by this trick and will watch—fascinated—as you torture your thumb!

The Haunted Paper Clips

You'll need: 2 paper clips
a dollar bill

Fold a dollar bill in an "S" shape and hold it in that position with two paper clips, placed as in the illustration.

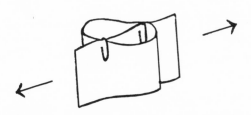

Now pull the ends of the dollar bill in opposite directions quickly. The paper clips will jump into the air and hook together!

You Have a Broken Finger

If you are tricky enough with your fingers, not only can you stretch your thumb, but you can even seem to break off your index finger.

Illus. 1

First, hold your hands as shown in Illustration 1. Then place your bent thumb right up against your index finger, which you have also bent. Now you need to cover up the spot where your thumb and index finger touch. Do this simply by placing the index finger of your upper hand over that place (see Illustration 2). This makes it look like a whole finger, even though it is just the combination of one thumb joint with one index finger joint.

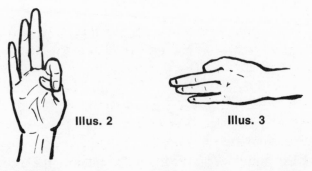

Illus. 2   **Illus. 3**

Now quickly slide the hand with the thumb-part away, without changing the position of any of your fingers (see Illustration 3). Your friends will think that your finger has actually broken off!

Before they can recover from their shock, slide your hands back together. The "broken" finger is together again! Then stretch out your finger normally and rub the "wound." Your puzzled spectators will try to figure out how you did it—so they can do it themselves.

The Disembodied Finger

Hold your index fingers horizontally a few inches in front of your eyes so that they don't quite meet—say, about half an inch apart (as in the illustration).

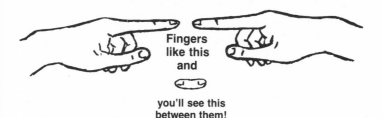

Fingers
like this
and

you'll see this
between them!

Focus your eyes on a spot farther away than your fingers—so that your fingers look blurry. Suddenly, in the space between your fingers, you'll see a new disembodied finger—short and fat with a nail on each end. Don't focus on it or it will disappear. Move your fingers closer to your face—or farther away—or closer to each other, and you can make the finger larger or smaller. If you're squeamish, turn your fingers so that your nails face away from you. Then the blob will look more like a floating sausage.

You Have a Hole in Your Hand

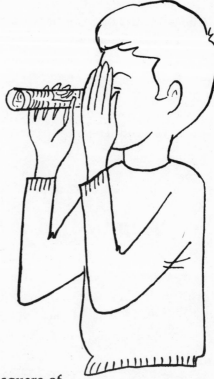

You'll need:
a newspaper square of
about 9 inches (23cm)
scissors
tape

Not only do you have a hole in your hand, but you can even look through it. Hard to believe?

Roll the square of newspaper into a tube about one inch (2½ cm) in diameter. Tape the free end of the paper to the inside of the tube.

Take the tube in your right hand and hold it to your right eye so that you can see through it easily.

Now raise your left hand, palm facing you, until it is a few inches in front of your left eye, with your little finger touching the side of the tube. Open both eyes and look straight ahead. You'll see a hole in your hand!

You Can Be a Human Pretzel

The following feat requires great flexibility of your arms. If you have long arms, you should be able to do it easily. The idea is to make a loop with your arms and stick your head through it.

Follow these steps:

1. Hook your fingers together, as shown in Illustration 1.

Illus. 1

2. Keeping your fingers clasped, slip one elbow into the bend of the other, so that your arms hold each other. (You should not have to release your fingers.)
3. Your arms now form a noose through which it is possible to stick your head (see Illustration 2).

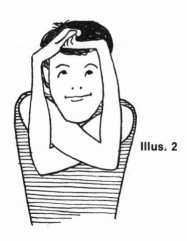

Illus. 2

Try it! While you're doing this, don't release your fingers. They should still be together when they're behind your neck.

4. Now slip your raised arms down slowly over your ears until your head peeks out of the loop made by your arms.

With a little practice, you will be able to demonstrate this at high speed.

You Can't Open Your Eyes

Tell your victims that, after you give them certain instructions, they may close their eyes—but they will not be able to open them again until you say the word.

The instructions are simple: Keeping your head straight forward, lift your eyeballs so that you're looking up at the ceiling. Don't move your head.

Then tell them to shut their eyes. As long as they keep looking up, it's physically impossible for them to open their eyes. When you're ready, just tell them to look down.

You Can Make People's Hair Stand on End

Blow up a balloon and rub it briskly on some fur or woolen cloth. You can use your sweater to produce a very effective charge of static electricity in the balloon. Then pass the balloon over the hair of your friends. Up it stands! Strangely enough, most people don't feel anything when their hair is attracted toward the balloon, so let someone hold up a mirror for them.

Incidentally, both pet cats and dogs show signs of uneasiness when the balloon is held close to their coats!

The Frankenstein Monster and the Invisible Man

The Invisible Man doesn't look invisible to you? Close your left eye. Keep your right eye focused on the Frankenstein Monster and move this book back and forth in front of you. At one point the Invisible Man will disappear completely.

Why? Because moving the book back and forth, you eventually find your blind spot—the spot where the optic nerve leaves your eye and there are no nerve cells to register an image. If you use both eyes as you look at the Frankenstein Monster, you won't have a blind spot, because the image from your left eye will make up for the blank in your right.

3. Unbelievable Feats

Stunts you never thought possible—amazing, astounding, but so simple to do—you'll find a dozen of them in this chapter. You don't need any special equipment to do these tricks, just ordinary everyday objects that you have around the house—and you don't have to develop any special skills. In fact, these tricks more or less work by themselves!

You Have Strange Power
Over Eggs

You'll need: 2 eggs (or 4, if you want to do an
encore)
2 glasses full of water
A pen
A spoon
Salt
A drinking straw or funnel

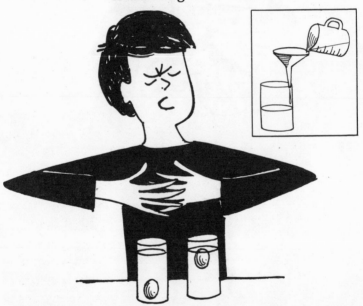

Announce that you're going to reveal the strange
power you have over eggs. You then produce two eggs
(fresh or hardboiled, it makes no difference—but hardboiled may be safer) and two glasses of water.

Ask someone in the audience to write the word "sink"
on one egg, and another person to write the word
"float" on the other.

Now tell your friends that these eggs will do just what they are told.

Saying this, place the "sink" egg in one glass and the "float" egg in the other. Do it gently, with a spoon. The "sink" egg will sink to the bottom of the glass and stay there. When you place the "float" egg in the glass, wave your hand mysteriously over the glass and say a few masterful things to the egg. The "float" egg will sink to the bottom—and then slowly rise to float on or near the top!

If your friends think there is something special about the eggs, produce two more and perform the stunt again, letting any skeptic write the words this time. If they think there is something peculiar about the water, take a sip from the top of each glass, or let them do it.

HOW IT IS DONE: The glass on the left is plain water, and the egg sinks in that. But the glass on the right contains salt water (in a strong solution) at the bottom with a layer of fresh water on top. The fresh will not mix with the salt water if you pour it on top through a straw or funnel and let it slide down the side of the glass. Just an inch or less of fresh water on top is enough. You make the salt solution by dissolving the salt long ahead of time in a glass and letting it stand. Then pour the solution into a fresh drinking glass so that no salt grains are visible at the bottom. Test with the egg to be sure the salt mixture is strong enough before adding the fresh water. And make sure, before performing the trick, that the glasses look alike.

You Can Carry a Column of Water

You'll need: A glass of water
A drinking straw

Place the straw in a glass of water and suck at the straw. When the water reaches your mouth, place your finger on the top end of the straw as you remove it from your mouth.

Keeping your finger in position, raise the straw from the glass. Trapped inside the straw—and held there by upward air pressure—is a slender column of water. You could walk around with it, if you wanted to, or run with it.

Now release your finger from the end of the straw, allowing air to come in the top of the column. The water will run out of the straw. Make sure the glass is underneath to catch it.

EXTRA: Do you have another straw? Try drinking water from the glass with both straws—except leaving one of the straws *out* of the glass. Water won't come up through *either* straw.

The reason? Normally, when you suck on a straw, you create a vacuum, which is what sends the water up to your mouth. By using the second straw you destroy that vacuum.

You Can Crawl Through a Narrow Paper Hoop

You'll need: A strip of paper about 24 inches (60cm) long
            Glue
            Scissors

You can crawl through a narrow paper hoop without tearing it.

The exact size you make your hoop depends on your size. A strip of paper about 24 inches long should be big enough for most 8- 12-year olds. If you're older, make it just an inch or two longer. The approximate diameter of the 24-inch hoop will be about 7 or 8 inches (20 cm).

Does it sound impossible for you to crawl through it? It would be, except that this is a trick. Only you will be able to do it—to the amazement of your friends.

HOW IT IS DONE: Before you paste the hoop together, give the paper strip a half twist. Your hoop should *not* look like Illustration 1, which is simply a pasted hoop. It should look like Illustration 2. A mathematician named Moebius once found out that a strip with a half twist doesn't fall into two parts if it is cut apart lengthwise. Instead—with this "Moebius strip"—you get a hoop twice the size!

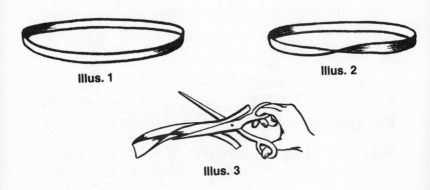

Illus. 1

Illus. 2

Illus. 3

Try this amazing thing. Cut the hoop lengthwise with your scissors. Now the hoop is large enough for you to crawl through it easily without breaking it. No one will guess what you did in making the hoop—they'll just think you're a sloppy worker!

You Can Crawl
Through a Playing Card

You'll need: An old playing card
Scissors

This extraordinary trick has been handed down from parents to children for centuries.

Take a playing card that you don't want to use again. Fold it lengthwise, as in Illustration 1. Make a series of cuts, as shown in Illustration 2.

Illus. 1

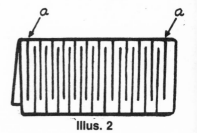

Illus. 2

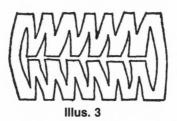

Illus. 3

Then cut the folded side from *a* to *a*. When you unfold the card, you get a structure which spreads apart to form a large ring! It is surely big enough—if the cuts are close together—to let you slip through!

You Can Lift an Ice Cube without Touching It

You'll need: Ice cubes
A bowl of water
A string 6 or 7 inches (15-18 cm)
long
Salt
A spoon

Challenge your friends to lift an ice cube out of a bowl of water on a string without touching the ice with their fingers or the spoon. Some of them will try to loop the string under or around the slippery cube. Others will be completely baffled.

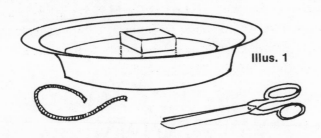

Illus. 1

How It Is Done:
1. Dip the string in the water until it is thoroughly wet.
2. Place one end of it across the top of the ice cube.
3. Sprinkle a spoonful of salt along the line of the string, allowing the salt to fall on both ice and string (see Illustration 2).

When the salt strikes the ice, it will melt it a little (you know how salt is used to melt ice on the streets and

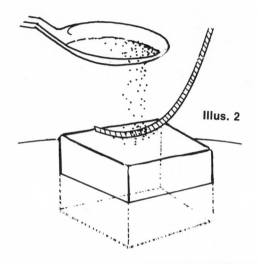

Illus. 2

sidewalk in winter?) and form a coating with the water in the string. As the water re-freezes, it joins in a strong bond with the string. Then you simply pull on the string and lift the ice cube out of the water.

**Illus. 3
When the ice freezes again, it traps the end of the string.**

You Can Turn a Glass of Water Upside Down without Spilling It

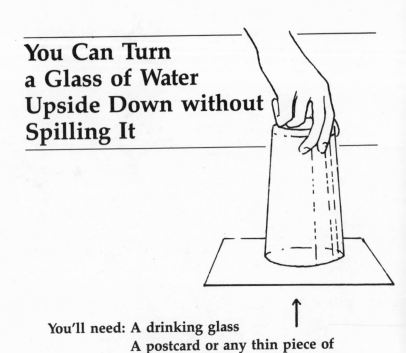

You'll need: A drinking glass
A postcard or any thin piece of cardboard with a glossy surface

Fill a smooth-rimmed drinking glass to the very top with water and place the postcard or cardboard on top of the glass. Press the card gently against the rim of the glass with your left hand, while you pick up the glass in your right hand and turn it upside down.

Now remove your left hand from the card carefully and—behold! The water stays in the glass in midair! In spite of gravity, which, you'd think, would drop both the water and the card to the floor, the card sticks to the rim of the glass and holds the water in.

What you've just achieved is the result of air pressure. Since there's almost no air at all inside the glass, the air can only press upwards on the underside of the card. That supports the water.

If you do this trick indoors, do it over a pail or sink. One clumsy move can result in a pretty wet floor.

Hanky Panky

You'll need: A handkerchief (or tissue or paper towel)
A large bowl, filled with water
A glass

You can plunge a handkerchief into a bowl of water without its getting wet! That's right, and you really have to try it to believe it!

Stuff the handkerchief (or the paper towel or tissue) into the bottom of the glass. Now plunge the glass straight down into the bowl or pan full of water, as in the illustration. Then pull the glass back out. The hanky is dry!

How can this be? When you plunge the glass straight down into the bowl of water, an air bubble forms in the glass. It's that bubble that keeps your hanky dry.

Knot That Way

You'll need: A string about 20 inches (50cm) long

Place the string on a table. Ask your friends to hold one end of the string in each hand and tie a knot—without letting go of the string.

Now you can sit back and watch them struggle. No matter how hard they try, they won't be able to tie a knot without releasing at least one hand.

Then you can demonstrate how to do it. Cross your arms—as shown in the illustration. Bend over the string

and grab the ends in your hands. As you straighten up, by uncrossing your arms you will have tied a perfect overhand knot.

44

Levitation

Four of you can lift even the heaviest person off a chair and into the air with only one or two fingers each. There is no gimmick to this feat. You really can do it and it's as easy as it looks!

Let one of the group sit in the chair. Then the four of you who will do the lifting stand at the corners of the chair. At a signal, you each take a deep breath and hold it. Then two of you put one or two fingers under the knees of the person in the chair, and the other two players put their fingers under the person's arms. Still holding your breath, you lift the person out of the chair and up into the air as if he or she weighed almost nothing at all! It is holding your breath that is the key to this feat. Don't let your breath go until the person is back in the chair.

You Can Defy Gravity

You'll need: A pitcher (or a large drinking glass with straight sides—or one that is wider at the bottom than at the top)
A small ball (such as one you'd use to play "jacks")

This trick involves carrying a small ball in a pitcher (or a large glass). Put the ball on the table and cover it with the empty pitcher. Challenge your friends to carry the ball from that table to another table without touching it and without turning the pitcher right side up.

Impossible? Actually, it's very simple to do. Just start making a circular motion with the pitcher so that you hit the ball and gradually get it to make the same circles as the pitcher itself. By doing this, you create a force (centrifugal force) which will press the ball against the inside of the pitcher. Now—without stopping the circular motion—you should be able to lift both the pitcher and the ball. As long as you keep the ball rotating inside the pitcher, it won't fall out, even though the pitcher is upside down.

Whether you use a pitcher, a glass or a vase for this trick, the container must have straight sides or, preferably, be wider at the base. Centrifugal force causes a ball to find the largest possible circle in which to rotate. As a result, in a pitcher or vase which is larger towards its base, the ball will be drawn up safely inside.

Then you can take a few careful steps and put the circling pitcher down on the other table. You have moved the ball without touching it.

Wings

Stand in a doorway and, with the back of your wrists, push hard against the door jamb. Keep pushing for at least a minute, with all your strength. Then walk through the doorway. Your arms will lift up and out—like wings—involuntarily! It's a weird feeling, having your arms lift up without your doing anything to cause it. Actually, it's only a reaction to the muscular pressure you were exerting when you were pushing against the doorway. But it does make you feel as if you're about to take off!

You Can Double Your Money

The fastest way to double your money is with a pencil! You don't believe it?

Take two identical coins and put them on the table in front of you, an inch or two apart. Now stand a pencil between them, and hold it with its point on the table.

Focus your eyes on the point of the pencil—not on the coins. Move the pencil toward you. It will suddenly appear that there are three coins on the table—and then four!

Don't get too happy about this, because as you move the pencil back and forth, there will be a moment in which you'll see only one coin in front of you (see page 32), but that won't last too long.

How is it that the coins multiply? It's the same principle as with the Disembodied Finger on page 27. You're not focused on the coins, so the images produced don't come together.

You Can Walk a Tightrope

You'll need: A pair of binoculars
A rope (clothesline will do)
about 20 feet (6m) long

Have you ever wondered what it's like to walk a tight-rope—many feet up in the air? Here's your chance to find out! Put the rope down in a straight line on the floor or outside on the ground. Then start to walk on it—just as if you were actually walking the tightrope—heel to toe—but as you walk, look through the "wrong" end of a pair of binoculars so that everything looks very far away. Even though you're actually walking on the ground, you'll feel as if you're a mile up in the air!

Why do you get that sensation? Your sense of sight is much stronger than your sense of touch. So even though you can feel the ground beneath your feet, your brain is getting an altogether different message from your eyes—and the message is "Look out!"

4. Sneaky Numbers

Even if you don't care anything about math, you'll be fascinated by number tricks once you give them a try. The tricks here are some of the best you'll ever find. They range from old classics to sleek new stunts that you need a calculator for. They're all mystifying, and your friends will be dying to know, "How do you do it?" Don't tell them. . . .

The Three-Digit Miracle

Take any 3-digit number, 197 for example.

Write it backwards:	791
Subtract the smaller number:	− 197
Total:	594
Now write the total backwards:	495
and add it:	1089

What's so miraculous about that? No matter *what* 3-digit number you use, you'll *always* come up with 1089!

Note: If you get the number 99 as the "total" number, look out. Remember, it isn't 99 at all, but 099. So when you write it backwards, write 990. For example:

112 is the number you pick	112
Write it backwards and subtract	211
the smaller number:	− 112
Total:	099
Write it backwards and add it:	990
	1089

The only numbers that won't work are numbers that are written the same way backwards and forwards, such as 141, 252, 343.

If you want to see how you can use this to perform other tricks, see page 70.

How Old Are You?

Try this one on your friends!

1. **Write down the number of the month in which you were born.**
2. **Multiply by 2.**
3. **Add 5.**
4. **Multiply the total by 50.**
5. **Add the magic number. (The magic number varies from year to year.**
   In 1984 it is 1434;
   in 1985 it is 1435;
   in 1986 it is 1436;
   in 1987 it is 1437, and so on)
6. **Deduct the year you were born.**

The last two digits are your age.

HOW IT IS DONE: What you're doing in Steps 1-4 is forcing your friends to come up with a figure that ends in the digits 50. Once you have that—and you add the "magic number," the last digits of that figure are the digits of the current year. Then it's a simple matter of deducting the year of birth and coming up with the victim's age. For instance:

Your birth month:	7
Multiple by 2:	14
Add 5:	19
Multiply by 50:	950
Add the magic number 1434 (if it's 1984)	1434
	2384
Deduct the year you were born:	1968
(your age)	16

The Secret Number (Easy)

People who are good at math won't have much trouble figuring out why this trick works. Others will be completely baffled. Tell your friends that you're going to read the numbers in their minds, if they do what you tell them.

1. **Ask them to think of a number, but *not* to tell it to you.**
2. **Tell them to double that number (mentally or on a calculator).**
3. **Multiply the result by 5.**
4. **Ask for the result.**
5. **Knock off the zero on the end, and what remains will be the number that your friend started with.**

For example, your friend may have selected the number 7. Doubling it makes it 14 and multiplying it by 5 makes 70. Why does it work? Because doubling the number and then multiplying it by 5 is just the same as multiplying by 10. When you take off the zero, of course, you have the original number.

The Secret Number (a Bit Harder)

If that was too simple for your friends, try this. Tell your friends that you'll guess two numbers at a time.

1. **Ask them to think of two numbers from 1 to 9, but *not* to tell you what they are.**
2. **Select *one* of the numbers and multiply it by 5—**
3. **Add 7—**
4. **And double the result.**
5. **Add the other original secret number.**
6. **Subtract 14.**
7. **Tell you the result.**
8. **It will be a 2-digit number—and each digit will be one of the secret numbers.**

For example, if someone thought of 2 and 9 and took 9 first, it would go like this:

$$9 \times 5 = 45$$
$$+ \ 7$$
$$52 \times 2 = 104$$
$$+ \ 2$$
$$106$$
$$- \ 14$$
$$92$$

Just as in the easy version of this trick, you're asking your friends to multiply the original number by 5 and then by 2 (by 10 altogether). The 7 is thrown in just to confuse them: After doubling it, you get them to subtract it by taking off 14. When the second number is added to 10 times the first one, you naturally get the two secret numbers.

Who's Got the String?

Number all the players in the group and ask them to tie a string on someone's finger while you leave the room or turn your back. Offer to tell them not only who has the string, but which hand and which finger it's tied to.

Ask one of the spectators to make the following calculations for you:

1. **Multiply by 2 the number of the person with the string.**
2. **Add 3.**
3. **Multiply the result by 5.**
4. **Add 8 if the string is on the right hand. Add 9 if the string is on the left hand.**
5. **Multiply by 10.**
6. **Add the number of the finger (the thumb is #1).**
7. **Add 2.**

When you're told the resulting number, mentally subtract 222. The number that remains gives you the answer, beginning with the right-hand digit.

For example, suppose the string is on the left hand, third finger of Player #4:

Player's number (4) multiplied by 2	8
Add 3	11
Multiply by 5	55
Add 9 for left hand	64
Multiply by 10	640
Add finger number (3)	643
Add 2	645
Subtract:	− 222
	423

The right-hand digit (3) stands for third finger.

The middle digit (2) stands for the left hand (1 would be the right hand).

The left-hand digit (4) tells the number of the person.

When the number of the person is above 9, the *two* left-hand digits indicate the number of the person.

Number Wizard

You are the number wizard.

Ask your friends to choose any number from 1 to 10.
Then tell them to add 8 to that number (keeping it secret).
Double it.
Divide it by 4.
Subtract half of the original number.

"The answer is 4," you say. And you are right! Even though your friends haven't told you a thing about their numbers!

If you had told them to add 6 to the original number, the answer would have been 3.

How does it work? The answer is always half of the number you tell them to add—everything else cancels out.

Try this one:

"Take a number," you say. "Add 7, double it, add 16, double it again, divide by 4 and subtract 15. Now you each have the number you started with."

Baffling? Still, it's not difficult to figure out. All the doubling, dividing, adding and subtracting equal out: You have really done nothing to change the original number.

Magic Number

There actually is a magic number which you can multiply with lightning speed in your head. The number is 142,857.

Pass out paper and pencil to your friends and yourself and show them that your paper is blank. You will use it only to write down the result.

Now ask your friends to multiply 142,857 by any number from 1 to 7. Then ask them—one at a time—to tell you any *one* figure in the result.

Suppose the third figure from the left is 5. You'll know immediately that the entire total is 285,714. You'll also know that the multiplier was 2.

Suppose the fourth figure from the left is 4: then you know the total is 571,428 and the multiplier is 4.

Do you get it? Every possible total of this magic number, when multiplied by 1 to 6, results in the same series of digits, but it begins at a different point. Multiply them out if you want to check, or run them through a calculator. If you know the position of any one digit in the sequence, you'll be able to write down the total correctly.

In the example above, when your friend told you that 4 was the fourth figure, you put down 428 at the end of the total, and 5, 7 and 1 in front, according to the sequence.

How do you know what the number 142,857 was multiplied by? Look at the last digit you write down. If it's a 4, you know the multiplier must be a 2 (since $2 \times 142,857 = 285,71\underline{4}$). If it's a 1, you know the multiplier must be 3 (since $3 \times 142,857 = 428,57\underline{1}$). If it's an 8, you know the multiplier must be 4, and so on. That last digit is different for each multiplication.

Wait a minute, you say—the only multipliers mentioned were 1 through 6, but at the beginning of this trick it said you could multiply with any number from 1 through 7. You're right: If you multiply the magic number by 7 you get another magic number:

999,999!

More about the foxy 142,857 on page 72.

Amazing Addition

With this fascinating trick you can add large numbers with remarkable speed and accuracy.

Ask your friends to write down two rows of numbers, each containing five digits, such as:

1st row: 34658
2nd row: 46829

Now you put down a third row of figures:

3rd row: 53170

Ask your friends to put down a fourth row:

4th row: 62353

And you write a fifth row:

5th row: 37646

Then you look at the figures a moment, write on a small piece of paper, fold the paper and give it to one of the spectators. You ask your friends to add up the numbers and call out the answer. When they figure it out, ask for your slip of paper and unfold it. There—for everyone to see—is the correct total.

HOW IT IS DONE: You work your calculations while

you're putting down your rows of figures. When you write the third row, make each of your numbers total 9 when added to the number *just above it*—the number in the 2nd row. Ignore the top row. When you write the fifth row, make each number total 9 when added to the number in the fourth row.

Now you can figure out the grand total very quickly from the *first* line: Just subtract 2 from the last number of the first line (8) and place the 2 at the front of the first line. The column total is this number.

Let's go over that again:

Friends:	34658
Friends:	46829
You:	53170
Friends:	62353
You:	37646
Total:	234656

EXCEPTIONS: If your friends write a *first* number

that ends in either 0 or 1, you need to mentally reverse the first and second row of figures. When you put down the third row, put down numbers that total 9 when added to the numbers in the *first* row. Ignore the second row until you get to the grand total. Follow the same procedure with the fourth and fifth rows. But figure the grand total of the column by using the *second* line— subtracting 2 from the last number and placing 2 in front of the first number.

Friends:	34650
Friends:	46929
You:	65349
Friends:	62353
You:	37646
Total:	246927

The Answer Is Always Nine

You'll need: A pocket calculator (or at least paper and pencil)

This sneaky stunt can be the basis for magic tricks and mind reading tricks of all kinds. Because when you go through the calculations, you always come out with the same number—9. There are many ways to do it.

This is one way:

1. **Put into your calculator any number from 10 to 99. (Your friend chooses 28.)**   28
2. **Reverse the digits.**   82
3. **Subtract the smaller number from the larger one. (82 − 28 = 54)**   54
4. **Divide by the difference in your original two digits. (In this case, the difference is 6: 8 − 2. So 54 divided by 6 = 9)**   9

It's good to have other ways to get to the number—so that you can repeat the trick without anyone's realizing you're really doing the same thing over and over.

Here's another way:

1. **Choose a number (567134, for example).**   567134
2. **Scramble it up, any way at all.**   <u>341765</u>
3. **Subtract the smaller number from the larger one.**   225369
4. **Cross-add the digits until only one is left.**
   (2 + 2 + 5 + 3 + 6 + 9 = 27
   2 + 7 =   9)   9

Or you can do it this way:

1. **Pick any number of up to 7 digits. (Your friend picks 4751)**   4751
2. **Multiply by 10.**   47510
3. **Subtract your original number.**   <u>4751</u>

    42759

4. **Divide by your original number. Result:**   9

Or this way:

1. **Pick any number of up to 6 digits.**
   (Your friend picks 4751)   4751
2. **Multiply by 100.**   475100
3. **Subtract your original number.**   <u>4751</u>

                                           470349

4. **Divide by 11.**   42759
5. **Divide by your original number.**
   Result: 9

Pretty boring trick, you might think, always coming up with that number? Wrong! First of all, your friends don't know that you "forced" them to come up with that number. Second, they have no idea that you know the number they have in their calculators or on their papers. And they probably won't figure that you *could* know—unless they're math buffs or know this trick. And most important, once you know what the number is, you are in complete control of the trick from that moment on. You can maneuver your friends into coming out with any number you want—if you work it all out in advance.

For example, let's say that your friend Steve's address is 182 River Road, and you decide you want Steve to come out with that number after all his calculations are over. After Steve has the 9 in his calculator, you might give him the following instructions:

(in Steve's calculator)	9
Add your grade in school. (You know Steve is in the eighth grade.)	8
Result:	17
What would you rather have $1000 or $1? Add the figure you'd like to have.	1000
Result:	1017
Subtract the last four digits of your telephone number. (You know Steve's number ends in 0822.)	0822
Result:	195
Subtract your age. (You know Steve is 13.)	13
The result is your street number:	182

Another good way to perform this trick is to write down the "182" prediction on a slip of paper before the trick begins and hand it to one of your other friends. Then have Steve do all the calculations and ask the spectator to read the prediction out loud.

You can make this trick look even more astounding. Instead of asking Steve to choose a number and going right into the steps that lead you to the "9," you can lead him on a wild goose chase through all kinds of silly—or personal—or general questions. For example:

1. Put into the calculator your date of birth: (You *don't* know Steve's date of birth, but no matter.)   211971
2. Multiply it by the number of people in your family (3).   635913
3. Subtract your lucky number.   13

                635900

4. Add your best friend's phone number.   5532716

                6168616

5. Subtract the number of beans in a bean bag.   500

                6168116

6. Subtract your phone number.   5559112

                609004

7. Add the number of your close friends.   2

                609006

8. Subtract the number of your enemies.   1

                609005

And then start the trick:

9. Scramble up the number now in your calculator.   560009
10. Subtract the smaller number from the larger one.   48996
11. Cross-add the digits until only one is left:
   $(4+8+9+9+6=36)$
                $(3+6=9)$ Result: 9

At this point you could go on with other questions that you know the answer to (for any result you want)—or you could stop—with 9.

Your Calculator Is Calling

**You'll need: A pocket calculator (or at least
pencil and paper)**

This simple trick is especially good for displaying
your friend's phone number (the last four digits) or address. And you'll notice that sneaky number here
again—1089 (you saw it earlier on page 52).

Suppose the last four digits of the telephone number
are 3823. Before the trick, secretly subtract 1089 from
this number:

$$\begin{array}{r} 3823 \\ \underline{1089} \\ 2734 \end{array}$$

Now ask your friend to do the following:

1. **Choose a number between 100 and 1000.** 235
2. **Reverse the numbers.** 532
3. **Subtract the smaller from the larger (532 − 235).** 297
4. **Do you now have a number between 100 and 999? (In the case, the answer is yes, so proceed as follows.)**
5. **Reverse the digits and add.** 792
   1089
6. **Add 2734 (the number you located before doing the trick).** 2734
   3823
7. **Does this number have any special significance to you?**

Your friend will have to admit it is his or her own telephone number.

There are two things to keep in mind while you do this trick. Look at Step 4. If your friend says no, the number in the machine is *not* between 100 and 999, substitute the following Step 5, instead.

Alternate Step 5: Reverse the digits, put a zero on the end, and add.

For example, if the number your friend had was 99 (it can't be lower than that), reversing the digits and putting a zero on the end would bring it to 990. 99 plus 990 equals 1089.

The one other possibility is that Step 4 will lead your friend to a zero. This would happen if your friend picked a number such as 101 or 202. Make sure that you're not starting with this type of number. One way to make sure is to tell your friend to select a number in which all the digits are different.

Mad Multipliers

You'll need: 2 pocket calculators (or paper and pencil)

Once you can force a number on your victim, you can perform all kinds of calculations and make up all sorts of tricks. Try this trick:

1. **Select any number between 2 and 6.**	5
2. **Multiply it by 1001.**	5005
3. **Multiply it by 111.**	555555
4. **Multiply that by 9.**	.4999995
5. **Divide by 7.**	714285

Does that last number look familiar? It's the "magic number" you saw before on page 60, or a variation on it. And as you found out before, if you do this trick with the number 2, you'll get 285714. If you do it with 3, you'll get 428571. If you do it with 4, you'll get 571428. If you do it with 6, you'll get 857142—always the same numbers, but in different sequence.

Now you can get your friends to select whatever number you want by telling them to take:

the lowest digit	**(1)**
the lowest even digit	**(2)**
the sum of the 2 lowest digits	**(3)**
the lowest even digit doubled	**(4)**
the middle-sized odd digit	**(5)**
the sum of the 2 lowest digits × 2	**(6)**
the highest odd digit	**(7)**
the highest digit	**(8)**
the sum of the 2 lowest digits × 3	**(9)**

Since you already know what digit your friends will pick—when you give one of those instructions listed above—you can carry them through some really involved calculations, and you'll already know the answer. If your calculator has a memory, you can do these involved calculations first, put them aside in memory, and then retrieve them later for more hocus-pocus.

* * * * * * * *

Now try this. Tell your friend to pick a secret number:

1. **Pick any number from 100 to 999.**   138
2. **Multiply it by 1001.**   138138

The number will always duplicate itself, side by side.

* * *

You can work this stunt in reverse:
1. **Pick any number from 100 to 999.**   537
2. **Duplicate it side by side.**   537537

In order to get back to the original number you would divide by 1001, but you want to be trickier than that. The number 1001 can be made up from 3 other numbers multiplied by each other—7 × 11 × 13. If you want your friend to come out with "13":

3. Divide by 7.	76791
4. Divide by 11.	6981
5. Divide by your secret number.	13

* * * * * * * *

Or if you would prefer to have your friend come out with 77, you could use the following steps instead:

3. Divide by 13.	41349
4. Divide by your secret number.	77

* * * * * * * *

Or if you want the secret number left:

3. Divide by 7.	76791
4. Divide by 11.	6981
5. Divide by 13.	537

If you want a 1 left:

6. Divide by your secret number:	1

* * * * * * * *

To do the same trick with a 2-digit number, ask your friend to select any number from 10 to 99 and to put it into the calculator three times, next to each other. This is the same as multiplying by 10101. This time you'd be dividing by 3, 7, 13 and 37. Try it:

1. **Select any number from 10 to 99.**   68
2. **Put it into your calculator 3 times**
   next to each other.   686868
3. **Divide by 3.**   228956
4. **Divide by 7.**   32708
5. **Divide by 13.**   2516
6. **Divide by 37.**   68

* * * * * * * *

And you can do it with a one-digit number, too. That would be the same as multiplying by 111, and you'd have to divide by 3 and 37.

1. **Select any number from 1 to 9.**   8
2. **Put it into your calculator 3 times,**
   next to each other.   888
3. **Divide by 3.**   296
4. **Divide by 37.**   8

The Number Is 43,046,721

You'll need: A pocket calculator (or paper and pencil)

This stunt works well for a friend whose age you don't know. First memorize the number 43,046,721, or write it on a slip of paper and put it in your pocket.

Then tell your friend to do the following:

1. **Put in your year of birth.**
2. **Subtract 3.**
3. **Add your age.**
4. **If you have not yet had your birthday this year, add 1. If your birthday is past, skip this step.**
5. **Subtract the current year.**
6. **Add 6.**
7. **Square the amount in your calculator.**
8. **Square the amount *now* in your calculator.**
9. **Square whatever amount you have in your calculator *now*.**
10. **Square whatever amount you have in your calculator *now*.**

Then tell your friend the answer—or bring the paper out of your pocket and show it around.

HOW IT IS DONE: When your friend put in the birth year plus age this year and subtracted the current year, nothing remained. All that your machine contained was $-3 + 6 = 3$. Knowing there will be a 3 in the machine, you can carry out any calculation you please, like this one for 43,046,721.

5. Mind-Reading Tricks

All kinds of mind-reading tricks are included in this chapter, from the sly kind with one of your friends in cahoots with you, to the type that is based on real clues that you can pick up by observing one of the players. Others are based on pure logic. All of them are easy to learn and mystifying in performance.

The Mysterious Temple

THE EFFECT: You leave the room while the group thinks of a number from 1 to 5. When you return, you walk around the group, pressing your hands to the temples of each of the players. Feeling their heads, you get "thought waves" from them and—by the time one round is completed—you announce the number the group had in mind.

HOW IT IS DONE: You will always guess the right number because you're not guessing. You have a spy or "partner" working for you. The spy clenches and unclenches teeth while you are pressing his or her temples. If the number is 3, the spy clenches teeth three times. That way you get the correct "thought wave."

Feel your own temples as you clench your teeth, and you'll see that this movement causes a ripple which you can feel easily.

Anyone who doesn't know the trick will think you're performing miracles!

The Mystic Circle and the Mystic Cross

THE EFFECT: You announce that there is a telepathic bond between you and your assistant. It starts working when you draw the mystic circle and the mystic cross. Then your assistant leaves the room. You point to one of your friends and say you will "send" the person's name to your assistant. When your assistant returns, he or she immediately points to the person and says, "You are the one."

HOW IT IS DONE: You draw the mystic circle by tracing a large circle on the table or on the floor with your finger. As you do it, you say, "This is the mystic circle," and then you wait for a moment, until someone speaks. You and your assistant have decided ahead of time that the first one to speak will be the person whose name you "send." Then you trace the mystic cross (inside the circle), saying, "And this is the mystic cross."

PERFORMANCE TIPS: If too many people talk all at once after you draw the mystic circle, you can say to your assistant, "You're not in the mystic circle—you're not getting my message, are you?" Your assistant will say "No," and you can start again.

Don't worry about what will happen if no one speaks. Someone always does!

Nose-Reading

Nose-reading is more limited than most mind-reading techniques, but it has its uses. With nose-reading, you'll be able to tell which hand holds the coin—or the candy or the prize or whatever—when someone asks you to choose between two clenched fists.

Start by telling your victim—say, Kathy—to hold both hands together in front of her body, making sure you can't see which one is holding the object. Then, when you say the word, Kathy is to stretch both arms out toward you (separated by at least an arm's length) with closed fists. And all the while she must concentrate hard on the hand with the object in it.

If Kathy is doing her job, you'll know which hand has the object right away. Her nose will tell you. At the moment she separates those hands and thrusts them out, her head will move—very slightly—in the direction of the hand with the object. Just keep watching the tip of her nose to pick up the movement.

ESP Takes a Trip

This is a good follow-up to the Mystic Circle and the Mystic Cross, proving that you and your assistant can work your ESP in several ways.

THE EFFECT: Your assistant leaves the room while a spectator—let's say, Lisa—decides on one article of clothing which she will take on a trip. When your assistant returns, you ask about several articles of clothing. Your assistant eliminates everything but the one piece of clothing that Lisa has selected.

HOW IT IS DONE: Before the act begins, you and your assistant decide on a color. You agree that the object you ask about immediately *after* you ask about something of that color is the one that is "going on the trip."

Let's say that the code color is white. And the object Lisa picked is her jeans. You say to your assistant:

"Kate is going on a trip. Can she take her shoes?"

"No," says your assistant.

"Can John take his eye glasses?"

"No."

"Can Marie take her blouse?" (Marie's blouse is white.)

"No."

"Can Lisa take her jeans?"

"Yes."

PERFORMANCE TIPS: You can vary this act by changing the color that you work with. Let it be white the first time, for example, red for an encore, and blue if you do it again.

Or skip the colors altogether. When you open the door to let your assistant in for the guessing part, be careful about the number of fingers you hold against the door. Whatever number you put there will be the number of the correct question. For example, if you put four fingers on the door, the fourth question will be the one to answer "yes" to. This limits you to ten questions, but that's more than enough.

Tricky Thumbs

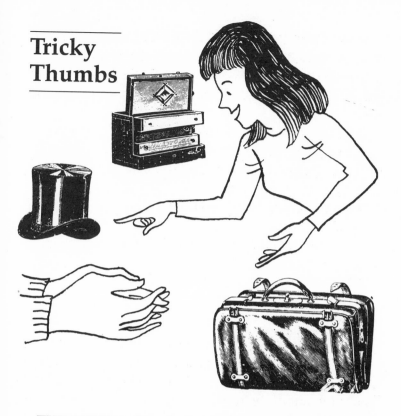

THE EFFECT: You leave the room while the other players place three objects on the floor or on the table. They decide which object they are going to concentrate on. When you return, you study the objects very carefully. Then you announce which one the group is thinking about.

HOW IT IS DONE: Another player is secretly in cahoots with you. While you pretend to study the objects carefully, you are just covering up a sneaky look at your partner's thumbs.

If the object is the one on the right, your partner's thumbs are crossed so the right one is over the left.

If the object is the one on the left, your partner's left thumb is crossed over the right one.

If the object is the one in the middle, both your partner's thumbs are held together side by side.

Be sure to practice this ahead of time with your partner so that you get the "left" and "right" of it straight.

The Classic Mind-Reading Act

You'll need: playing cards

In this classic mind-reading routine, your assistant—let's say, Ron—is the medium, and you pass along the message to him.

THE EFFECT: Blindfold Ron and sit him in a chair while you walk among your friends with a deck of cards. Let one of them select a card. Then announce that Ron and you have an amazing telepathic bond that will enable you to "transmit" to him the value and suit of the card your friend has selected.

You take the card, look at it hard as if memorizing it, and then ask Ron to tell you about it.

Ron starts slowly, but gradually the image "comes clear" and he names the card correctly.

HOW IT IS DONE: When you take the card from the spectator, you say the following words:

If the card is a Heart:	Thanks.
If the card is a Diamond:	Thank you.
If the card is a Club:	Okay.
If the card is a Spade:	All right.

Then you start "sending" the card to Ron, who has heard what you said to the spectator. Let's say the card is the Queen of Diamonds. When you take it from the spectator, you say "Thank you," and start "sending." Ron immediately knows the card is a Diamond. But he doesn't tell all he knows.

"I see the color red," says Ron.

If the card is in the lower range of numbers—between Ace and 6, you say nothing.

If the card is in the upper range of numbers—between 7 and the Queen—you say, "Yes," or "Right."

If the card is a King, you say, "Yes," or "Right," and then add more words—any words you want. In this case, Ron knows at once that the card is a King, and he says so without going on further.

Since the card is the Queen of Diamonds, you say just "Yes," or "Right," and Ron knows that the card is somewhere between the 7 and the Queen of Diamonds. But again, he doesn't tell all he knows. This time he reveals the part of the answer that he didn't tell before.

"It's a Diamond," he says.

If the card is the lower range of numbers—7, 8 or 9, you say nothing.

If the card is in the upper range of numbers—10, Jack, Queen—you say, "Yes," or "Right."

In this case, you say, "Yes," and Ron knows that the card is in the upper group, a 10, Jack or Queen.

"I'm getting a high number," Ron might say.

If the card is the first one in that group of three (the

10), you'd give a one-word answer, such as, "Yes," or "Oh?"

If the card is the second one (in this case, the Jack), you'd give a two-word answer, such as, "Go on," or "That's good," or "Are you?"

If the card is the third one (in this case, the Queen), you say nothing.

In this case, of course, you say nothing, and Ron will say, "The card is the Queen of Diamonds."

Here is a breakdown of the code:

> When taking the card:
> Heart: "Thanks."
> Diamond: "Thank you."
> Club: "Okay."
> Spade: "All right."

Lower	Upper	
A 2 3 4 5 6 Silence	7 8 9 10 J Q "Yes"	K "Yes" plus more words

A 2 3 Silence	4 5 6 "Yes"	7 8 9 Silence	10 J Q "Yes"

First card of group (A, 4, 7 or 10):   one word
Second card of group (2, 5, 8 or J): two words
Third card of group (3, 6, 9 or Q):   silence

Hot Cash

You'll need: 6 coins, all of the same denomination but with different mint dates on them

THE EFFECT: Six coins—all of the same denomination—are spread out on the table. Each one has a different date on it. While you turn your back, one of your friends—Anne—will select a coin and show it to the others. They will silently note the date on the coin and make sure it is different from the other coins on the table.

Then Anne will hold the coin up to her "third eye" (a spot in the center of the forehead about an inch over the bridge of the nose) for 60 seconds. She will then return the coin to the table. You go to the table, pass your hand over the coins and tell her the date on the coin she selected.

HOW IT IS DONE: When Anne holds the coin to her forehead, you tell her to press it hard to her third eye with her "psychic fingers," the three middle fingers of her left hand.

After holding it to her forehead for a full minute, Anne's coin will be hotter than the coins that are lying on the table. When you pass your fingers over the coins, most of them will be quite cool. The one that's warmer than the rest is the chosen coin. Then you just read off the date.

I've Got Your Number

You'll need: 7 square cards, each with a number on it, as described below.

THE EFFECT: You show the seven square cards to the group. One person, Mark, let's say, notes a number, and you place the cards face-down in a circle. You tap the cards in a jumbled way while Mark spells his number, mentally, letter by letter.

For example, suppose Mark spells "E-L-E-V-E-N," and on the final letter says, "Stop!" You turn the cardboard square up and, by an amazing coincidence, it is Mark's number—11!

HOW IT IS DONE: Each number is spelled with a different number of letters, so the count works automatically. The numbers on the cards are:

2—T-W-O
5—F-I-V-E
7—S-E-V-E-N
11—E-L-E-V-E-N
16—S-I-X-T-E-E-N
13—T-H-I-R-T-E-E-N
17—S-E-V-E-N-T-E-E-N

When you place the cards in a circle, you arrange them as follows:

2
7   13
16 11
17 5

Make the first two taps on any card, but on the third tap, hit the 2, so that if Mark is spelling "T-W-O," he will say, "Stop!" as he completes his spelling and you will turn up his card.

For the next tap, jump two cards clockwise, hitting the 5. The next jump is two more, to the 7, then to the 11, and so on around the circle, automatically turning up the right number on the word "Stop!"

PERFORMANCE TIPS: When you show the cards, don't say anything about spelling. Just say:

"Here are some cards with numbers from 1 to 20."

And you run through them, numbers up, saying, "And I want you to take one, look at it, remember it, and mix it with the rest, numbers down."

You hand Mark the cards, numbers down so that he can do this, while you turn away. Then you reach for the cards, saying: "Let me have the cards so I can go through them while you keep thinking of your number—just that number and no other. I'll try to catch your thought. . . . Now I have it!"

You don't have it, of course, but that gives you a chance to set your circle in the correct order.

You continue: "As I tap the cards, I want you to spell your number mentally, like 'O-N-E' for 1—or 'T-E-N' for 10—and on the last letter say 'Stop'!"

Go about your tapping slowly, as if you are concentrating deeply. This allows time for the spelling.

Instead of jumping two cards, you can move diagonally across the circle, as though you are drawing a seven-pointed star. This amounts to the same as jumping, but makes it look more like a jumbled, meaningless sequence.

The Nine Slips

You'll need: A sheet of paper with smooth edges
A pencil
A hat—or a deep bowl

THE EFFECT: You tear a sheet of paper into nine slips, all the same size. A spectator—Jean—writes any name on a slip, folds it, and drops it into a hat or deep bowl.

Now she writes other names on the remaining slips, folds them the same way and mixes them in the hat.

While Jean concentrates on the original name, you read through the slips one by one and finally announce the name that Jean has in mind!

HOW IT IS DONE: Be sure to use a sheet of paper with smooth edges. If necessary, cut any rough edges with a pair of scissors beforehand. Fold the paper into thirds—both ways—so it can be torn into nine equal pieces (see Illustration 1).

Illus. 1

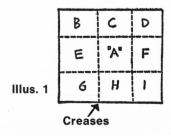

Creases

Do this neatly, so that the slips look alike, but one of them—the original center of the sheet—will be slightly different. It will have four rough edges, whereas every other slip will have at least one smooth edge (see Illustration 2).

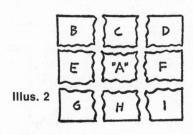

Illus. 2

Illus. 3
Drop the slips in the hat.

Illus. 4
Find the slip with all rough edges.

Hand Jean the slip with the four rough edges first, or put it on top of the others, so that she uses it to write the name she has in mind. More names are written on the remaining slips, but you can always pick out the right one by its four rough edges.

PERFORMANCE TIPS: Stress the fact that you're trying to catch one thought out of nine, and that the slips are merely incidental. Go through them one by one, name by name; then start over and stop on the chosen one. That makes it look like real mind reading.

"Reading" with Your Forehead

You'll need: A small square of paper for each
spectator
A pencil for each spectator

THE EFFECT: You give each spectator a small square
of paper and a pencil, telling them to write a word or
short sentence on the paper, and then fold it neatly in
quarters. You select one of the spectators to be your
assistant, and that player collects the folded papers and
gives them to you.

You take one of the papers and press it (still folded) to
your forehead. Then you announce the message and,
incredibly, it is the exact message that one of the spectators wrote.

You open up the paper to make sure the spectator is
telling you the truth. Can you do it again? (Sure you
can.)

You take the next paper and hold it to your forehead,
as if the message is going right through into your mind.
Then you announce the message. It is, word for word,

the sentence of one of the other spectators.

This goes on while you total up a perfect score.

HOW IT IS DONE: The assistant that you select is working in cahoots with you. Before the trick, you two decide what his or her "message" will be. And your assistant makes sure that paper is at the *bottom* of the pile that is given to you.

Then, when you take the top paper from the pile to "read" it mentally, you announce the message that you two decided upon in advance. Your assistant says, "That's mine! I wrote that!"

When you look at the paper to "check," what you're seeing is one of the *other* messages, one that belongs to someone else in the group. You remember it, put the paper aside and press the next message to your psychic forehead. When you announce the message, you report what you've just seen written on the previous piece of paper!

Each time you open a paper to "check" and make sure you got it right, you are reading the next message.

PERFORMANCE TIPS: Don't perform this trick more than once. The spectators might get suspicious about the fact that your assistant's message is always read first. But it's a mighty impressive trick the first time. Your friends won't be able to figure out how you did it unless they know the secret.

6. Card Tricks

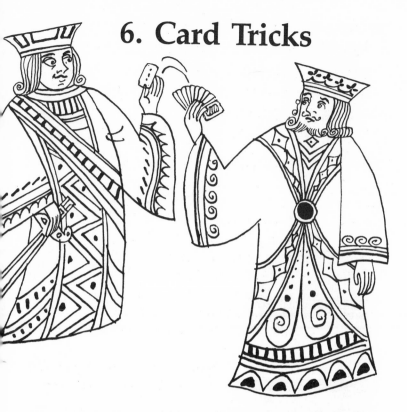

The tricks in this section are all simple to do. None of them call for sleight of hand. All you need, in most cases, is a pack of cards and you can start doing them immediately, as part of a magic act, or for your family and friends.

You don't need any fancy dealing or trick decks, but this is important: the more smoothly, the more neatly you handle the cards, the more effective your tricks will be. If you handle a pack of cards clumsily, people take for granted that your tricks must be easy; otherwise, they think, you couldn't do them. But when you shuffle the cards briskly and deal them rapidly, your friends will have enough confidence in you so that they will happily sit back and let themselves be fooled.

The Two Rows

THE EFFECT: You tell a spectator—say, Bill—to deal two rows of cards, each row containing the same number of cards, so that he'll have the number firmly fixed in his mind.

He can use any number of cards—from 3 or 4 to 20—in each row; it is entirely up to him. You are going to give him instructions on how to re-arrange the rows in various ways. While he is re-arranging them, you turn your back or go into another room (as long as he can hear you from there).

When Bill and you are ready, tell him to take away cards from either row, but to tell you *how many* cards he takes, and from which row, *top or bottom*.

After he does that, tell him he can do what he wants—take more cards from either row—or add cards, or transfer them from row to the other, as long as he tells you how many were moved and says which row—or rows are involved.

At one point, you suggest a number for Bill to take away, but he never tells you how many cards either row contains.

Then suddenly you say, "Stop!" And you name the exact number of cards that remain.

HOW IT IS DONE: The number of cards in each row *does not matter*, as long as the rows are equal at the start. For example, assume that Bill puts seven cards in each row:

TOP: * * * * * * *
BOTTOM: * * * * * * *

You don't see these cards, but you take a high number of your own—say 20—and imagine or visualize the rows as containing 20 cards each. Then you ask Bill to take away cards, add them, or move them as he chooses, but to tell you what he does. Like this:

He moves 3 cards from the bottom row to the top, and says so. That leaves the rows like this:

TOP: * * * * * * * * *

BOTTOM: * * * *

Working from your "key" number 20, you mentally move 3 from bottom to top, saying to yourself, "Twenty-three in the top row—17 in the bottom row."

Now, suppose Bill takes away 2 from the bottom row, stating that fact. He has:

TOP: * * * * * * * * *

BOTTOM: * *

You say to yourself: "Two from 17 leaves 15 in the bottom row—with 23 still in the top row."

Bill decides to add one card to each row. He announces that fact and performs the action, so that the rows stand:

TOP: * * * * * * * * * *

BOTTOM: * * *

Mentally, you add one to each of *your* rows, giving you 24 in the top row and 16 in the bottom row.

Now comes the important part: You tell Bill to count

the number of cards in the bottom row and take that many away from the top row. (Obviously, he doesn't tell you how many he is moving this time.) He takes 3 (the number in his bottom row) from the 11 cards in his top row, which gives him:

TOP: * * * * * * * *
BOTTOM: * * *

Meanwhile, you are doing the same thing with your imaginary rows, subtracting 16 (bottom) from 24 (top), so you have 8 cards in your top row.

Now you tell Bill to take away his bottom row entirely. That leaves him with a single row.

* * * * * * * *

You too eliminate your imaginary bottom row (16 cards) and that leaves you with a single row of just 8 cards, identical with the row now on the table!

From then on, you can let Bill add or subtract cards as he wants, providing he states the exact number in each case. You go right along with him, for you are both working with the same number.

Assume that he simply takes away four cards. He then has:

* * * *

You do the same and announce your final total: "Four!"

PERFORMANCE TIPS: First you tell Bill to deal a row of cards, and then another with the same number, so he has the number fixed in his mind. As he does it, you add: "It can be a small number or a large one, anything from 2 up to 20, but be sure you deal the same number twice—and don't change it—at least, not yet!"

Here you give him the impression that you are already beginning to "get" the number. Then you say:

"Now take away or add cards to either row, but tell me how many cards you move and what you do with them. You can simply move them from one row to the other, if you want."

With that done, you continue: "Now move a few more and tell me again. From these partial thoughts, I am trying to get a full impression."

After a few such moves (as already described), you say, "Stop! I think I have it. Just to make sure our minds are tuned, I want you to count the cards in the smaller row, without telling me. Take that row entirely away. You've done it? Good. Now take the same number from the other row, so as to fix it firmly in mind. Add a few more, or take some away, if you prefer, but this time, tell me how many. That's enough. I have it!"

You can do this trick with coins or straws or toothpicks, as well as with cards.

The Two Rows Encore

This makes a good follow-up to The Two Rows. The tricks are similar, but there is enough difference between them to throw observers off the trail.

THE EFFECT: Tell one of the spectators—Sally, let's say—to take an odd number of cards and put them down in equal rows. The extra card can go in either row. Turn your back while Sally lays out the cards.

The rows might be:

```
* * * * * *
* * * * * *
```

Now ask Sally to name a small number, less than the number of cards in either row. Suppose she says, "Five." You tell her to take 5 cards from the long row and put them aside. The rows will then stand:

```
  * *
* * * * * *
```

Next, tell Sally to count the cards in what is now the short row, and to take that many away from the other row, without telling you the number (which happens to be 2, in this case). This leaves:

```
        * *
        * * * *
```

Then téll Sally to take away the first row entirely and to concentrate upon the number of cards in the remaining row:

```
        * * * *
```

After much concentration and exchange of "brain waves," you name the number, "Four."

HOW IT IS DONE: This trick works itself. Your key number for the climax is *one less* than the number that Sally named at the beginning! In this case, Sally picked up 5, and that meant there would be 4 at the finish. If she had picked 3, there would have been 2 left, and so on.

PERFORMANCE TIPS: You need a few rehearsals in order to make this trick work smoothly and effectively. Play up the mind-reading angle at every stage. When Sally adds the "odd" card to one row, act as if you are "picking up" the number of cards even then.

After Sally chooses her number, continue to "concentrate." When you tell her to remove the first row, you can say, "Your mind seems to be going from one row to another. Take away the first row entirely. You've done that? I thought so. . . . Now count the cards in the one remaining row. Count them mentally, one by one. Fix on the final number and keep it firmly in mind. I am counting to myself now. One, two, three, four! That is the number!"

NOTE: If Sally picks the number *one* at the start and removes only one card, the rows will be the same and the trick won't work. If she says, "One," simply say, "That's too small. Let's make it larger." Or you can tell her to double it, and take two cards from the long row. Or, at the start, you can say. "Name any number above 1—but less than the number of cards in either row."

The Multiplying Cards

You'll need: A flat plate
20 playing cards

THE EFFECT: One by one you place about 10 cards on a flat plate and ask a spectator to count them. The spectator counts them and returns the cards to the table, but you shake your head and look doubtful. Then you ask another spectator to check the number of cards. You personally hand them to this volunteer. To everyone's surprise, there turn out to be twice as many cards as before!

HOW IT IS DONE: The illustration gives the trick away. You have hidden the extra cards under the plate. You hold them in place with your right hand, the same hand which is holding the plate. Using your left hand, you push the cards on top of the plate under your right thumb. Then, with your left hand, you take the plate, getting the two piles together. All the while, angle the plate forward so that no one can see the pile of cards under it.

PERFORMANCE TIPS: It will be easy to pick up both the plate and the concealed pile of cards at the same time if you place them both at the very edge of the table, with the cards hanging over the table edge, in fact.

The Rising Card

You'll need: A deck of cards which is still in the package

THE EFFECT: You show the audience an ordinary pack of cards, still in the package. Open the top of the package and hold the deck in your outstretched right hand. Say a bit of hocus-pocus over the pack and slowly a card slides up out of the box.

HOW IT IS DONE: Cut a slit about half an inch (15mm) wide and 1½ inches (35mm) long on the back of

When you cut a slot in the card box, you can make the cards "crawl" out of the box "by themselves."

the package (see the illustration). With your right index finger, push the card up.

PERFORMANCE TIPS: This trick works best when the pack of cards is not quite full. Be sure to follow up this trick rapidly with another one—or switch the package for an identical deck so that no one gets a chance to see the back of the pack.

X-Ray Eyes

You'll need: A deck of cards, still in the package

THE EFFECT: After you hand a deck of cards over to the spectators to be shuffled, you replace the deck in its package. You tell your friends that you will prove that you have X-ray eyes which can see right through the package.

Holding the pack of cards in your outstretched hand, you announce the suit and number of each card as you (or one of your friends draws it up slowly) out of the package. Hand it over to your friends for inspection. You do seem to have X-rays eyes.

HOW IT IS DONE: Actually, you have a little square "window" cut in the lower right corner of the back of the package. Don't make the window any larger than can be covered by your thumb, so you can show the back of the package to the audience. At the same time, make the window big enough so that you can see the suit and number, which are found in the corners of all decks of cards.

PERFORMANCE TIPS: Remember to insert the cards into the package so that the face side appears through the hole. Another good thing to remember is that an upside-down 6 looks like a 9, and vice-versa.

Mutus Dedit Nomen Cocis

THE EFFECT: Give the spectator, Robert, a packet of 20 cards to lay out on the table *face down* in sets of two. Then turn your back and ask him to select one of these sets of two, look at the cards in it, and remember them.

Other spectators can look at a set, too. If there are ten people watching, each one can look at a set of two and remember it.

Turning around now, you gather up the sets, keeping them together, and lay the cards out on the table, *face up* in four rows of five cards each.

"Which one or two rows are your cards in?" you ask Robert.

As soon as he points to the rows which house his two cards, you announce what they are. And you do the same thing for any other spectators who point out the rows their cards are in.

HOW IT IS DONE: This trick is based on code words, which you need to memorize. The words are "Mutus" (pronounced MEW-tus), "Dedit" (DEAD-it), "Nomen" (NO-mun), "Cocis" (COCK-us).

M U T U S

D E D I T

N O M E N

C O C I S

The layout—numbered by sets

1	2	3	2	4
5	6	5	7	3
8	9	1	6	8
10	9	10	7	4

When you lay out the cards, instead of just putting them down in any old order, you follow the letter pattern in the words. For example, you put the first set (two cards) down in the spots occupied by the M's—the M in Mutus and the only other M spot, and the M in Nomen. Then you put the second set of two cards into the spots reserved for the U's—both of them in Mutus. And so on for set #3: start with the T in Mutus and then go to the T in Dedit, and on until you have laid out all the sets.

So when you ask Robert to point out the rows (horizontally) in which his cards are located, it's a simple question of finding the two identical letters.

If Robert says both cards are in the first row, you know automatically that it is the set of U's in Mutus.

If his cards are in rows 1 and 2, you know he must have had the T's in Mutus and Dedit.

If they are in rows 1 and 3, he had the M's in Mutus and Nomen.

If they are in rows 1 and 4, he had the S-position cards in Mutus and Cocis.

If the cards are only in the second row, he had the D's in Dedit.

If they are in the second and third rows, he had the E's in Dedit and Nomen.

If they are in the second and last rows, they are the I's in Dedit and Cocis.

If Robert says his cards are only in the third row, he had the N's in Nomen.

In the third and fourth rows, he had the O's in Nomen and Cocis.

And, if they are just in the last row, he had the C's in Cocis.

PERFORMANCE TIPS: This trick works well only if you memorize the words thoroughly. Practice until you can lay out the cards in the four-word pattern with speed and assurance. Once you can do that, it's simple to remember the code when it comes time to find the sets. As you start placing the pairs, you can say, "I'll place these here and there, so they'll be all mixed up," but all the while, you are setting them down according to your formula.

For a repeat, it's a good idea to lay out the pairs differently. You can change the order of the words, and use other formulas, too, instead of Mutus Dedit Nomen Cocis. (Some of those are Latin words, but as far as we can tell, they don't have any secret meaning.)

Here are three other arrangements:

```
T A R O T
E N D E R
I O N I C
S C A D S

M O T O R
S H E E R
N I N T H
M I L L S

S A L A D
Z I P P S
T I T L E
O O Z E D
```

Card Under Glass

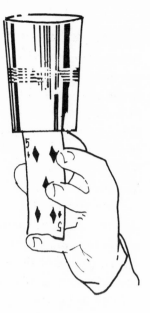

**You'll need: A plastic glass
One playing card**

THE EFFECT: You show both the front and back of a card to your friends. Then, holding the card between your right thumb and index finger (if you are right-handed), you carefully place a plastic glass on top of the card. You concentrate very hard to find the point of balance. At last you succeed and the glass balances on top of the card.

HOW IT IS DONE: The illustration reveals the secret. As you can see, your right index finger, hidden by the card, supports the glass.

PERFORMANCE TIPS: If you use a very small glass, you may want to try putting some water in it. This makes the trick all the more dramatic, but make sure the glass is not too heavy.

Do the trick above the eye level of the spectators, so they can't see your index finger at work.

Do As I Do

This classic trick will bewilder your audience, but it is easy to do once you learn to handle the cards in a convincing way.

THE EFFECT: You take two packs of cards and let a spectator—Joyce—choose either pack. You shuffle one pack and she shuffles the other.

To show that all is fair, you then exchange packs, so that each of you shuffles the other's cards. Finally, you hand your pack to Joyce and say, "From now on, do as I do, and let's see what happens."

You deal out your pack in three heaps on the table. Joyce does the same thing with her pack.

You lift the top card of the middle heap and peek at it. Joyce does the same, and you remind her, "I am remembering my card, so I want you to remember yours."

Now you gather the heaps and give your pack two or three cuts. Joyce does the same with her pack. Remarking that the peeked-at cards are now "well buried," you exchange packs again. Then you say:

"I'm going to look through your pack and take out the card that I found in mine. You look through my pack and find yours. Then we'll put them face down on the table."

Once you each pick out your cards, set the packs aside. Dramatically, you turn up the two cards. They are identical! By an amazing "coincidence," you have each taken the same card from a different pack!

HOW IT IS DONE: After a few shuffles and ex-changes, take a peek at the bottom card of the pack that you hand to Joyce. Here is one way to do that:

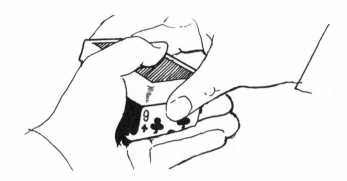

Let's say the bottom card is the 9 of Clubs. You take her pack and say, "Now do as I do."

Lift off about ⅔ of the pack and set it to the right. Then lift off the top third and put it farther to the right.

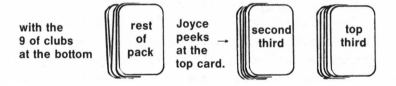

Joyce does the same with the pack you gave her.

Peek at the top card of the middle heap, but don't bother to remember it. Still keep thinking of that bottom card of the other pack. Pick up the left-hand heap of your pack, put it on the middle heap, and place both heaps on the right heap.

Joyce does the same with her pack. In the process, she plants the bottom card—the 9 of Clubs that you secretly noted—squarely on the card at which she peeked!

You cut the pack twice or three times, and chances are

the two cards will remain together. So after you exchange packs again, simply look through Joyce's pack for the 9 of Clubs, and remove the card just below it, say the Jack of Diamonds.

That will be the card Joyce looked at. Meanwhile, she is looking through your pack, finding the Jack of Diamonds and taking it out as you instructed. So the two cards turn out to be identical.

PERFORMANCE TIPS: Do this trick with confidence. If you miss a chance to note the bottom card, or if it gets lost in a chance shuffle, simply exchange the packs again and proceed from there.

Sometimes you may "spot" the bottom card of the pack that Joyce is shuffling. In that case, you don't have to note yours. Instead of exchanging packs, you would say, "Just put your pack on the table and cut it as I do mine."

Don't worry about which pack is which after the trick has passed the preliminary stage. Just refer to a pack as "your pack" or "my pack," according to convenience or the way it develops.

If Joyce starts to shuffle her pack after looking at her card, don't give up the trick. Just say, "That's good. Now let me shuffle your pack while you shuffle mine." At the same time, hand her your pack.

It generally takes a good shuffle to separate the chosen card and the "key" card above it, so chances are the trick will work anyway. If it misses, try again, preferably with *Do As I Do Again*, which follows.

Do As I Do Again

THE EFFECT of this trick is almost identical to the last one. You and Joyce shuffle the two packs and exchange them. Each of you notes a card and these, when drawn from the other's pack, are the same.

HOW IT IS DONE: During a shuffle, note the *top card* of your pack before handing it to Joyce. Then tell her, "Do as I do."

In this case, lift off ⅔ of the pack and carry it well to the right. Then lift off the top third of that heap and bring it back a short way, setting it between the other two, so that it becomes the middle heap.

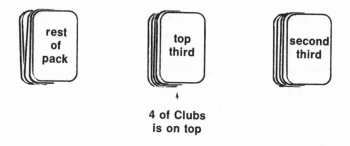

4 of Clubs
is on top

You do this with Joyce's pack. She does the same with yours. Now you say, "Look at the top card of the middle heap and remember it."

Joyce looks at the card you noted, say the 4 of Clubs, while you are peeking at a card in her pack.

Exchange the packs again. Joyce looks for her card in your deck, and you look for your card in hers. You both come up with the 4 of Clubs.

PERFORMANCE TIPS: This version has the advantage that the card is "forced" on Joyce, so the trick cannot possibly miss. Furthermore, you can include a shuffle in the routine after the top card of the middle heap has been noted by Joyce. You simply say, "Now do as I do and shuffle the pack thoroughly." Then you follow with the final exchange.

The best plan is to work the original *Do As I Do* and save the second version for a repeat. In the original trick, Joyce actually takes a random card from deep in the deck. The second trick depends on an odd handling of the heaps, which works best when you're dealing with a smart spectator who is looking for something else.

Double Dealing

This trick is based upon a neat but simple mathematical stunt, and it becomes a real puzzler when you allow the spectators to mystify themselves!

THE EFFECT: Give a spectator—say, Andy—a pack of cards and tell him to deal off any number—up to 20— while your back is turned. After he does that, tell him to deal another heap with the same number of cards, to make sure he doesn't forget the number.

Then tell Andy to deal a third heap of 10 cards, and then to gather all the heaps together and deal them into two separate piles, alternating left and right. He is then to pick up either pile. From it he deals the original number of cards onto the other pile.

Finally, Andy counts the remaining cards in his hand and concentrates on that number. You immediately announce the number of cards he is holding.

HOW IT IS DONE: The trick hinges on the third heap of cards you tell Andy to deal, the pile of 10. At the finish, he will have just half that number, so by announcing "Five," you are sure to be correct.

For example, suppose Andy deals off 8 cards. Told to deal the same number again, he deals off 8 more, making 16. Now you say, "Deal ten more." That brings the total to 26.

When Andy deals these cards into two piles, they will contain 13 cards each. From one of these, he deals the original number—8 onto the other pile. That leaves 5 cards, the number you proceed to name.

PERFORMANCE TIPS: Since the result is "set" beforehand, stress the fact that Andy has his free choice of any number. When you tell him to "Deal 10 more," do it casually, as though those extra cards do not particularly matter.

When you repeat the trick, change that number. Tell him to "Deal 6 more," and the final total will be 3. Tell him to deal 12 more, and the total will be 6, and so on.

Four-Heap Deal

THE EFFECT: You shuffle the deck thoroughly and spread it *face down* along the table so that a spectator—Dan—can remove any four cards, which he places face down in a row.

Gather up the rest of the pack and hand it to Dan. Then turn your back and tell him to turn up the first of the four cards and note its value: 1 for Ace, 2 for deuce, and so on. All the face cards (Jacks, Queens and Kings) count as 10.

On top of that first card, tell Dan to deal enough additional cards *(face down)* to total 12. For example, on a 7 he would deal 5 cards; on a 10 or a King, 2 cards.

Now Dan turns up the next card he placed in the row and repeats the process, and continues with the third and fourth cards. Here is a sample result:

**These cards start face down
and are turned up one by one.**

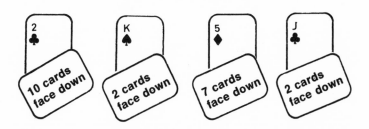

These cards remain face down.

Now you tell Dan to add the values of the face-up cards (in the illustration they add up to 27: 2 for the 2 of Clubs, 10 for the King of Spades, 5 for the 5 of Diamonds, 10 for the Jack of Clubs). Then he is to count down into the pack and turn up the 27th card. He is to look at it and remember it. Then you call out the name of a card, say "The Queen of Hearts," and it proves to be the chosen card.

HOW IT IS DONE: You need a pack of exactly 52 cards, so be sure to remove any Jokers beforehand. All you have to do is get a look at the bottom card after the shuffle—in this case, the Queen of Hearts—and the rest is automatic. (See page 111 for a way to sneak a look at the bottom card.)

For example, if four Aces were turned up, Dan would have to deal 11 cards on each, making 48 in all. Only four cards would be left in the pack. He would gather the 44 face-down cards, drop the 4 cards from the pack on top, and count down the total of the Aces, exactly four cards.

With four 10's or face cards, he would deal 2 on each, making 8 face-down cards and leaving 40 cards in the pack. He would gather up the 8 cards, drop the rest of the pack on top and count down 40 cards (the value of the 10's—or face cards).

Tell Dan he can gather the face-down heaps in any order he wants, and place the rest of the pack face down on the pile.

PERFORMANCE TIPS: It's a good idea to illustrate beforehand just what you want Dan to do. Deal a card face up, then add face-down cards to bring the numerical total to 12, saying that you will have him do that with several heaps. Show him how to gather the face-down cards and drop the pack on them.

Then shuffle the pack, spot the bottom card, and go right into the routine. If you are using this method to "force" the card, or as a mind-reading act, it is best to turn away as much as possible. But if you do it as a prediction, by writing the name of the bottom card on a folded slip of paper before Dan draws the four cards from the pack, you can watch the process and help in the gathering of the face-down piles.

As long as Dan does most of the dealing and is convinced that you could not have manipulated the cards in any way, the trick is 100 per cent effective.

The Great Silly Sentence Card Trick

No one will ever be able to figure out how you do this trick unless you tell them—or unless they've read this book, except for your partner—Sara, let's say—who goes out of the room while you set up the trick with your friends.

THE EFFECT: First you pick out of the deck all the Aces, deuces, threes and fours and put them aside. Then you lay out the rest of the cards in six rows of six cards each, all face up.

After Sara has left the room, you ask one of the spectators to select a card and name it aloud. When this is done, you call Sara back, say one silly sentence or phrase to her, such as "Dogs love spaghetti," and ask her to name the chosen card. Sara (ignoring you, and puzzling for a few moments) names the correct card.

HOW IT IS DONE: The silly sentence is a code, of course, and it is based on the following key:

(A) Animal (or Bird, Fish, etc.)
(T) Thing (anything inanimate, except a place)
(M) Male
(F) Female
(P) Place (anything from "the house" to Paris or the moon)
(N) Number

You and your partner, Sara, have memorized that sequence and will be using it as you look at the cards in each row. This is the way the cards will look to you:

Second Word

	Animal	Thing	Male	Female	Place	Number
First Word						
Animal row	AA	AT	AM	AF	AP	AN
Thing row	TA	TT	TM	TF	TP	TN
Male row	MA	MT	MM	MF	MP	MN
Female row	FA	FT	FM	FF	FP	FN
Place row	PA	PT	PM	PF	PP	PN
Number row	NA	NT	NM	NF	NP	NN

When you decide on a sentence for Sara, the first important word in it will tell her which horizontal row the card is in.

For example, if the selected card is in the top row (the Animal row), you might start the sentence with the word, "Dogs," or "Most lions," or "My canary," or any other member of the animal kingdom. The "animal" word doesn't have to be the first word, but it should be the first *important* word.

The next important word in the sentence should tell Sara which vertical row the card is in. This of course will pinpoint the chosen card. For example, if you want to tell Sara that the card is the first one in the first row (Animal-Animal), you might say something like, "Dogs like ducks." If you wanted to tell her that the card was the second one in the first row (Animal-Thing), you might say, "Most lions sleep on couches." If it's the third card (Animal-Male), you could say, "My canary likes Billy Joel."

Your sentence doesn't have to be silly unless you want it to. You can try using sentences that sound as if you're not even paying any attention to the card trick, such as "Rover got Mother so mad today," (Animal-

Female); or "My dog needs to get picked up by 3:00," (Animal-Number).

PERFORMANCE TIPS: You can perform this trick any number of times. Your friends will realize the sentence is a code, but so many possibilities are open to you when you make up sentences, that few of them will catch on.

If any very sharp spectator does seem to be breaking your code, you and your partner may want to do The Diagonal Switch. Instead of describing the card the spectators pick, you describe the card that is one space over and one space down. For example, instead of describing the "Animal-Animal" card, you'd describe "Thing-Thing." Your partner, who expects the Switch, identifies the card, and then switches back to the correct card.

One way or another, you should be able to fool all of the spectators all of the time.

The Magician's Card Trick

This card trick is famous, and for good reason. It's fun to do; it works itself, and it's completely mystifying.

THE EFFECT: You let the spectators shuffle the cards. Then you deal the cards into small piles. The spectators choose three of those piles, turn two of them bottoms up, and you announce the value of the bottom card of the face-down pile. As always, you are right.

HOW IT IS DONE: After the spectators shuffle the cards, you take a card from the top of the deck. Let's say it's a 5. You start counting aloud as you put the card face down on the table: "Five," you say, and you continue dealing cards face down on top of it, counting "Six, seven, eight, nine, ten." Now you have a pile of six cards.

You show your friends the next card on the top of the deck; let's say it's an 8. You put it face down on the table (as you did with the 5) and say, "Eight," and then deal more cards on top of it, counting, "Nine, ten," so you have a pile of three cards.

You go on in this way, making each pile count to 10 from wherever the first card starts.

Let's say the next card on the top of the deck is a 10. Since you can't put any cards down on top of it, you place it in a discard pile. You do the same with any Jack, Queen or King that you turn up. By the time you get to the last pile, you may not have enough cards to put down to get to "Ten," so you put the entire incomplete pile into the discard pile.

Now let the spectators examine the piles that are left. They can even move them around (but without changing the order of the cards in any pile). If there are any piles with less than four cards in them, put them in the discard pile.

Tell the spectators to select three of the piles and to give the others to you. Put the rejected piles in the discard pile.

Then take the discard pile in your hand and count off 19 cards. Put them on the table, off to the side.

Ask a spectator to turn up two of the three remaining piles so that everyone can see the two bottom cards. Let's say that one of the cards is a 5 and one a 4. Add those numbers together—9, and deal off nine cards from the pile that you're still holding in your hand (the discard pile minus nineteen cards).

Count the cards you're still holding in your hand. However many you have—that will be the number of the card on the bottom of the face-down pile. If you have five cards, the card will be a 5; if you have two cards, it will be a 2, and so on.

PERFORMANCE TIPS: After you demonstrate this

trick once, your friends may argue that you saw all the bottom cards at the start of the trick, so the odds were good that you remembered them. Of course, you didn't memorize the cards—or even notice them. But if you want, show your friends how to deal out the original piles themselves. Turn your back while they do it, and *then*—knock 'em dead with your magic!

Index